Toes in the Sand

My Journey from Domestic Engineer to Entrepreneur

By Lisa Carol Pulliam

pursue His purpose
with passion,
Lisa Pulliam
2016

Toes in the Sand: My Journey from Domestic Engineer to Entrepreneur

Toes in the Sand: My Journey from Domestic Engineer to Entrepreneur

1. Christianity 2. Entrepreneurship

E-book Version: Kindle

ISBN-10: 0692671137
ISBN-13: 978-0692671139
CHRISTIANITY: Entrepreneurship

Dedication

This book is dedicated to my grandmother Marge. We call her Sitti, which is Arabic for grandmother. Recently we celebrated this remarkable woman's 94th birthday. My mom, dad, aunts and uncles surprised her with a weekend getaway that any 94 year old would enjoy. We took her to see the legendary Willie Nelson in concert! Watching her eyes sparkle as Willie played his guitar and sang to his heart's content, was an experience I will never ever forget.

My Sitti is a strong, passionate, and faithful woman. She and my grandfather, Eddie were married 47 years and together they have four happily married children, eleven grandchildren and twenty great grandchildren! My grandfather passed away in 1988 and we all miss him dearly, but Sitti finds joy surrounded by her family. She especially loves when we gather together for a celebration of any kind. She has suffered through loss of loved ones, and overcome health issues, but her attitude is always one of grace and gratitude. When I call her on the phone to say hello, she responds, "Lisa B!". After she asks how Chris and each one of the kids are doing, I finally have a chance to ask her, "How are you feeling Sitti?" to which she responds, "Feeling great baby!"

Her attitude inspires me to always be thankful for the blessings in life, and to not dwell on the things you cannot change. Sitti, I love you with all my heart. I treasure every moment with you and will always be grateful that you are my Sitti.

Table of Contents

In appreciation

Chris, you invited me to share in this adventure called life with you. You have always encouraged me to be me. Nothing less and nothing more. For this I am forever grateful. I love you.

Emily, Robert, Patrick and Carol Ann, the joy you have brought to my life is indescribable. The Lord has great plans for each of you. May you always walk in His footsteps. Welcome to the family, Brandon.

Mom and Dad, you have demonstrated grace, laughter, unconditional love, encouragement, and a marriage that is committed 'til death do us part. Thank you. I Love you both dearly.

Krissy and John, Hannah, Matthew, Thomas and Rachel, we treasure our summer vacations at the beach with you every summer as far back as we can remember. Krissy, you are an amazing mother, wife and woman of God. I am blessed to have you as my sister and true friend.

John Jr., Katie, Trey and Tyler, I love you and look forward to every time we can be together. JBJ, you have become an incredible father, husband, and a successful entrepreneur. You inspire me.

Bob and Lucille, Grams and Papa, you have loved me as your own daughter since I first met Grams in her hand painted poinsettia sweatshirt. I love you both dearly.

Aunt Marilyn, as my godmother, you have always been encouraging and supportive throughout my life. I admire your ambition and the generosity with which you have lived your life. I love you.

Leslie Hart what would I have done without your friendship this past year? I have enjoyed digging my toes in the sand with you and I treasure every conversation. May God bless you richly as you have blessed me, my friend.

Laurie Morrow, how grateful I am that our paths crossed years ago when you and Don came to Arkansas. We set out on a journey in ministry and motherhood together. You and Don have enriched our lives tremendously and we enjoy each and every moment we spend together.

Esther Spina, almost two years ago sitting at Snoopy's and eating dinner watching the sunset over the ocean, you inspired me to finish writing my book. I am grateful for your mentorship and encouragement through my journey as an entrepreneur.

Amy Applebaum, your coaching has been invaluable to me these past two years. You have challenged me to grow as a woman, a mom, a wife and an entrepreneur so that I can make a bigger impact in this world. Thank you.

Connie Herr, you were not just my middle school math teacher, you lifted me up during a lonely time. You believed in me and reminded me that God had great plans for my life. I will always be grateful to you for caring.

Introduction

At the water's edge is where I want to be. Whether I'm sitting beside a crystal turquoise pool, overlooking a lake at a breathtaking sunset, or sitting in a lounge chair with my toes in the sand I feel closest to God when I am near the water. Yes, I am at my best when the sun is beaming its golden warmth on my shoulders and miles of deep blue waters roll before me. Ahhhh. I just know there will be salty sea air in Heaven.

Gazing at a beautiful body of water, I feel more alive than I do anywhere else. I feel peace, joy and a deep sense that God is so much bigger than any obstacle I may be facing at that time. During these treasured moments, I find myself reflecting, praying, and thinking about the Creator who crafted these magnificent colors of blue, gold, and pink, and gave us His creation to enjoy.

Growing up in Fort Worth, Texas meant the beach was only half a day's drive away! As a girl I anticipated our annual family summer vacations down on the Texas' coast. The quaint fishing town of Rockport and the laid back "Jimmy Buffet" beach town of Port Aransas were highlights of my childhood and teenage years. I remember getting burned to a crisp as my younger sister Kristen and I laid out in the sun from morning to evening. We splashed in the salty water to cool our burning skin off then lathered one another with aloe vera gel at night. Sandcastles, of course. We did not have a care in the world (other than dealing with a painful sunburn!). Most mornings, dad and our little brother, John, would hop up while it was still dark outside and tippy toe out the door for a few hours of early morning pier fishing. Mom, Kristen and I would wake up in the mornings around 9 am to the sound of the men returning from their fishing excursion. If they had been lucky, we knew dinner was going to be "John Jr.'s Fresh Catch of the Day!"

At least one evening during every summer vacation, the dinner destination was Charlotte Plummer's Seafare Restaurant. Charlotte Plummer's sat on a pier overlooking the bay of Rockport, TX. After a long hot day in the sun, we couldn't wait to get ourselves cleaned up, and hurry over to this popular restaurant beloved by locals and tourists alike. Dad would greet the waiter or waitress and immediately order the largest platter available of "peel 'em & eat 'em" shrimp. We three kids would giggle that the menu actually said "peel 'em n eat 'em" and not "boiled shrimp"! While we waited for this mouthwatering delicacy to arrive, we stood, noses pressed up against the windows, and watched the shrimp boats returning with huge nets of fresh shrimp. Dad would explain to us that the shrimp we were about to eat had been minding their own business at the bottom of the bay just a few minutes prior! Mmmmm, I can taste those fresh shrimp now.

Memories of these family vacations bring a smile to my face and a yearning in my soul to grab my flip flops and sunglasses, and head to the coast. After a childhood filled with times like these with my family together at the water's edge, I was hooked...a true lover of the water. I should have been a mermaid!

When I turned sixteen, I realized that I could be at the water's edge and earn money! So I earned my Red Cross Lifeguard certification and worked long, sweltering days for two summers at our local community pool. In college, I completed another Red Cross course called Water Safety Instructor. This gave me the certification to start teaching swim lessons to children. Now I could be IN the water and earn money! The summer after graduating from college, I sought out a summer position as the Waterfront Director at an Episcopal Youth camp in Connecticut. This camp was nestled in a beautiful wooded area and I spent the summer by the lake overseeing all boating and swimming activities for hundreds of children and counselors. My dream job!

As I grew older, water became a sanctuary for me—there's a peace in, on and near the water. I sense God's presence stronger there than anywhere else. My dream home overlooks a lake. I don't live in it yet, but I will someday soon. I imagine myself morning after morning, enjoying coffee on the deck, listening to the quiet morning sounds of the birds, and finding peace gazing out at the placid water. I imagine my children and future grandchildren coming to visit for the weekend, swimming together in the pool, taking the grandkids for a ride in the pontoon boat, grilling hamburgers in my outdoor kitchen while watching the breathtaking sunset over the water, my loved ones all around me. I feel closest to Him near the water. Water makes me feel alive.

I am in awe that He who made all of this beauty made me too. He not only made me, He loves me deeply, as deep as the deepest ocean and as wide as the bluest sky. The water reminds me that He has a plan and purpose for my life far greater than what I am living right now. I am often struck by the thought that if I will only get out of His way, He will do marvelous things through me to impact the lives of others and to leave my mark on this world.

Dr. John Maxwell is one of my favorite authors and speakers. I have had the privilege of hearing him speak several times at our company's annual conference. When that man takes the stage, he owns it. He speaks with conviction, and weaves humor and love into his message. In his book "The 15 Invaluable Laws of Growth", he says, "There are two great days in a person's life: the day you were born, and the day you discover why." May I just admit something to you right now? I am still discovering why. Are you? I am on a journey along with you to discover why I am here. What does the Lord have for me to accomplish? What impact am I supposed to make?

Deep within me is a desire to live life to the fullest, to not miss one single adventure, to work hard, to play hard, and to spread His joy to everyone I meet. Not only am I on a journey to discover my purpose in this life, but I have a desire to help others along the way to discover theirs. In his book, Dr. Maxwell quotes a poem called "Dream Big." I hope it speaks to your heart as it does mine:

If there were ever a time to dare,
To make a difference,
To embark on something worth doing,
It is now.
Not for any grand cause, necessarily -
But for something that tugs at your heart,
Something that's your aspiration,
Something that's your dream.
You owe it to yourself to make your days here count.
Have fun.
Dig deep.
Stretch.
Dream big.
Know, though, that things worth doing seldom come easy.
There will be good days.
And there will be bad days.
There will be times when you want to turn around,
Pack it up and call it quits.
Those times tell you that you are pushing yourself.
That you are not afraid to learn by trying.

Let's dig our toes into the sand. Let's laugh. Let's do some soul searching. Let's consider "why." I believe you were created with greatness inside of you, but it's hiding behind the security of what is comfortable...hidden inside the busyness, distractions, and life pulling at you from every angle. Sometimes with my toes in the sand I ponder this question: When I become old (halfway there) and gray (definitely there, just hiding it) and I am nearing the end of my life, what will I wish I had spent more time doing? Could I have made a bigger difference in this world?

Now is the time, my friends, to dig deep and discover the life God has for you.

Chapter 1
You're Going to Be a What?

I remember our first date like it was yesterday. I was a hair-bow-wearing sorority girl in my junior year at Texas Christian University. He was a third-year seminary student at Brite Divinity School at TCU, located on the "other side of University Drive." We had met on campus a time or two through mutual friends. We had even served as counselors at a large summer camp for kids in Missouri two years before, but that was it...a brief introduction, a smile, and a hello.

In January 1989, I was back on campus having just returned from a semester abroad in London, England. I was the type that was always looking for the next adventure and my semester in Europe had been just that. I had survived living on my own in a foreign land for four months, maneuvering my way around this enormous city on the "tube". I lived in a *Friends*-like" situation with six flat mates from around the United States, travelled across Europe and somehow came away from this semester with nine college credits! (How I ever made it to class in the midst of "pub-life" is beyond me!) During this semester I realized that this world was much bigger than my own "bubble life" at my university. I met people with all kinds of accents and religious beliefs, and backgrounds. What a fascinating time I had that semester and how the Lord used it to help me grow up and discover that I was quite an independent and adventurous young lady!

So I returned to TCU for spring semester junior year with a refreshed, broadened and "more mature" outlook on life. I reconnected with friends on campus and set my sights on graduation date: May 1990. I had three semesters plus a summer to go. Buckle down; let's get this thing done. There was a great big world out there brimming with opportunities… and it was calling my name.

About two months into the semester, I received a phone call. It was from that "older" guy in seminary, named Chris Pulliam. He asked me if I would like to go with him to see the play "Oklahoma" where his best friend had a leading role? I was zoned in on Graduation 1990 I and wasn't looking to date anyone at that time. But it sounded like a fun evening so I said Yes. Wait a minute. Wasn't this the guy from whom my London roommate had received a letter while we were overseas just a few months before? They were friends at TCU. I remember Kristin receiving his letter that day, and, after reading it, looking at me with this strangely pleasant expression as she said, "Lisa, I can *totally* see you with Chris Pulliam." Perplexed, I looked back at her and said something which resembled, "I don't think so!" All I could think of was that Chris Pulliam was way too mature for me and the phase of life I was in. Wasn't he in seminary? (What WAS that anyway?)

I guess I said yes to his phone call because a few nights later, my handsome, 6'2" date with dark auburn hair and several stitches across one eyebrow picked me up at my sorority house. I was totally unaware that the first night of the rest of my life had begun. The play was enjoyable followed by a nighttime walk around the campus giving us opportunity to talk, laugh and begin to get to know one another. The stitches, he informed me, were from an 'elbow-above–the-eye hit' during an intramural basketball game - an athlete, handsome, and an older guy. He seemed so mature compared to all those goofy undergraduate boys I'd been hanging around, but who was he, and why had he asked me out? One more question nagged me, but I couldn't seem to muster the courage to ask it. It was a question I should have known the answer to, but somehow I didn't.

As he walked me back to my dorm, I finally gathered the nerve to ask it, "So…" I paused, "What does someone do when they finish (pause) seminary?" (Was I clueless or what?) Chris very patiently turned to me and replied, "I'm going to be a minister."

"A minister? (another pause) … of a church?" I asked.

"Yes, I'm going to be a minister of a church," smiled Chris.

At this moment, one thought flashed across my mind: the priests of the Episcopal church in which I was raised were all old, bearded men who wore clerical collars. This guy was tall and handsome with an athletic build. I just couldn't see him in a clerical collar nor a long-flowing black robe, nor could I picture myself dating (or God forbid, marrying) someone who wore one.

Chris must have noticed the "deer in the headlights look" in my eyes. The next few moments of conversation are a blur, but soon he was walking me to the door. I thanked him for the evening and once again pictured him wearing a clerical collar as he smiled and walked towards his car. Clerical collar or not, the next moment I found myself running up the stairs in the sorority house knocking on doors looking for someone who was home at 11:00 pm on a Saturday night. (Only pastors-to-be are home this early on Saturday night.) I had to tell someone about this wonderful guy I had spent the evening with. I found my friend Mindy and told her all about this wonderful man I had met. Something unexpected had begun.

At this moment you may be thinking, "How could she not have known what a seminary student planned to do with his life? I tell you, I was clueless. But this is a very true story as proof that I was *not* looking to marry a minister! Is any woman? Rich businessman with a red Porsche, yes! Pastor of a church, not on my radar screen at that time in my life, and I was a Christian! I had been very involved with a campus ministry called Campus Crusade for Christ at TCU where I had gone on my first mission trip to Mexico – a life changing experience! I had helped lead a sorority bible study group, had served as a Young Life Leader at a local high school and worked at Kanakuk Kamp for Kids in Branson, Missouri. All of these ministry opportunities had challenged me to grow me in my faith. God had used my college years to open doors of excitement and new growth in me and I had walked through them, but could He have possibly been preparing me for this?

So I waited for the call-back from Chris. We had this great first date, so I just knew I would be hearing from him the next day, but he didn't call. Tomorrow came and went again, no phone call. I began to question the connection I thought we had felt. A week later he called just to say hi. (*Why had he waited so long?)* My heart pounded like a drum as we talked on the phone. I found myself thinking about this guy all the time and hoping I would run into him on campus. (*What I didn't know then was that Chris's older and wiser sister had taught him the "play it cool" tactic. "When you like a girl," she had taught him in high school, "don't call her the next day after your date. Wait a few days. Make her wonder if you're going to call. Keep her guessing." Well, thanks, Anne. The "play it cool" tactic definitely worked on me!)*

A few phone calls and a month later our second encounter occurred. I was nestled into my upstairs cubby at the TCU library, munching on my yogurt-covered raisins and trying to stay focused on "Organizational Management." The TCU Library was built around a large, open-air atrium. Being truly social, I knew to perch myself where I could overlook the atrium and see all who came and went—after all how much focus does Organizational Management require? There he was. He was just arriving at the library, and what do you know, I was just leaving. So I scooped up my books and my raisins and headed down the stairs, just in time to see him looking up at me and smiling. I smiled back, of course, as we proceeded to exchange "Hi's" and "How are you's?" Then came the second date request, "Would you like to go to a Texas Ranger baseball game next Saturday?" Smiling even bigger, I accepted. We chatted a few more moments then said goodbye. As I got into my car, I glanced into my rearview mirror to check my appearance. What I saw next was horrifying! What was that black glob between my two front teeth? A piece of raisin? Oh no! Please God tell me this wasn't here a few minutes ago as I bared all my teeth to Chris in the library.

Well, the couple of conversations Chris and I had were nice. He sure is handsome and kind. He makes me smile. However, at any minute he will be calling to cancel our date to the Ranger game. It's over now, a raisin between my the teeth, smiling big, practically running down the stairs at the TCU library to accidentally run into him, trying not to let it show how excited I was to see him. A goofy, immature undergraduate sorority girl thinking I even have a chance with Chris Pulliam, four years my senior, planning to be a pastor of a church. It's never going to happen.

However, it did happen. We went to the Ranger game and we began dating. Two years later we were married. The Lord of Lords had a plan, and a raisin in the tooth was not about to stop it. Several years earlier, the Lord had taken hold of my heart. I had given my life to Him and promised to walk with Him, to listen to Him, to learn to read and study His Word, to ask Him to lead me and guide me, and the Lord had lead me here - to marry Chris, and be a pastor's wife, a role about which I knew nothing.

Lisa's Lessons from Shore

*Do you plan, and dream, and believe you have it all figured out? Do you search and look far and wide for who or what you think you want? There is One who knows you better than you know yourself. He knows your needs and your desires and He is **for** you. Therefore, seek His plan and trust in Him with all your heart.*

"Many are the plans in a man's heart, but it is the Lord's purpose that prevails." Proverbs 19:21

"Trust in the Lord with all your heart and lean not on your own understanding. In all your ways acknowledge him and He will make your paths straight." Proverbs 3:5-6

Chapter 2
Saddle Up Your Horses

During my 25 years of marriage to Chris, I have never met another pastor's wife who set out to marry a minister. Though I have searched high and low for a class entitled, "How to Not Only Survive but Thrive in your Role as Minister's Wife," no such preparatory class existed for this particular role in life. Yet it is a role which comes with great responsibility and great sacrifice. It thrust me into the limelight, alongside my husband, and did the same for our marriage, our children and our life in general. This role comes with great and varying expectations placed on me by hundreds of people (many of whom I hardly know). Although I did not seek it out, I found myself in this position wondering, "What am I supposed to be doing here?", "Can I live up to these expectations?" and sometimes, "Why can we not just be a normal couple like everyone else"?

We were living in Houston enjoying a blissful first year of early marriage where Chris was an Associate Minister, and I was working in a non-profit organization. Life was fun. I showed up for worship Sunday mornings. I helped him with the youth on Sunday nights, and that was it. No great expectations on me yet, just a church of wonderful loving people who had thrown us a huge wedding shower. Some of these loving people had even driven five hours to Fort Worth to attend the wedding of their adorable young bachelor Associate Minister and his bride. Life was good. We were newlyweds! The stress-free, double income, no kids, just having fun being together stage. And to put icing on the cake, we only lived 45 minutes from Galveston Island! On Sundays after church, we would pack a picnic lunch, throw our bathing suits in a bag, and head to the island for a leisurely Sunday afternoon in the sun and sand. Ahhhhh, this was the life.

One day, the phone rang. A church in Arkansas, only one and a half hours from Chris's hometown, was searching for a new pastor, a Senior Minister. They asked him if he would like to interview for this position. "Why?" I thought. "We're having fun here in Houston. Things are going well; I like my job. We have a cute little apartment, and I'm only a few minutes from the beach! Plus, we've only been married one year. And all my family is in Texas. Besides, I've never even heard of this town before. Where in the world is Rogers, Arkansas?" Chris pulled out a map, and with a pen and a smile, pointed to a tiny dot in the corner of the state. "It's right there. Come on. Let's go check it out. I think you'll love it. "

We travelled to this beautiful church in Arkansas to meet with the search committee. I was so nervous. Chris was pumped up and ready to go. He was familiar with this church and this town and couldn't wait to show it to me. As we ascended into the rolling hills of Arkansas, the multi-colored speckled mountainsides of rich fall foliage surrounded us and seemed to welcome us to the area. "Lord," I prayed silently, "I am so nervous and scared. I feel like I'm just along for the ride. What are the people's expectations of me going to be? What if I cannot live up to them? I need you right now Lord. Help me. Guide us into Your will. Calm my fears as we venture into the unknown."

The committee wanted to meet with us together, then with Chris alone. I don't remember much about the afternoon. Only that we sat around a large table with six or eight members of the congregation asking Chris questions. Occasionally a question would come my direction, and I would take a deep breath and smile (and hope that I didn't have a raisin in my tooth!).

There was one question I remember well: "Lisa, do you by any chance play the organ?" I paused as I tried to discern whether he was serious or kidding. "No," I replied, (I knew I should have taken piano lessons more seriously as a child.) The committee chuckled as if to say, "We like you, and whatever gifts you bring to the life of this congregation will be welcomed." I had a sense that this was a church that would accept me as I was - full of inabilities and insecurities. The church extended the call to Chris to come and be their Senior Minister, and it began - our first great adventure. We were 24 and 28 years old, newlyweds, clueless, yet full of faith that the Lord was at the steering wheel of this 1984 Honda Accord and that we were following Him into the life He was calling us into.

Lisa's Lessons from Shore

Sometimes life throws you a curve. You have it all figured out and everything is just like you want it. Then out of the blue, seemingly overnight, your plans change without your permission. What do you do when this happens to you??

A mentor of mine, Esther Spina, has taught me a very valuable lesson in life. I have heard her say this over and over again through the years:

"You have to learn to discipline your disappointments." Sometimes a change of plans can become your next adventure!

"Saddle up your horses, we got a trail to blaze. In the wild blue yonder of God's amazing grace. Let's follow our leader into the glorious unknown... this is a life like no other, whoa, this is the Great Adventure..." Steven Curtis Chapman

Chapter 3
A New Baby and a True Friend

Let's face it. Marriage itself is a great adventure. Two people usually with polar opposite personalities, quirky habits, drastically different upbringings, and an unmatched set of luggage... I mean baggage... joining their lives together and then expecting a lifetime of peace and harmony. Add the life of living in the public eye to the already stressful circumstances every marriage faces, and we could have a recipe for disaster.

When I said "yes" to marrying Chris, I said yes to Chris - not his profession, not his calling—just to him. I said yes to the love we shared and to the plan God had for our lives (whatever plan that would be). I said yes to the belief that together we would step out in faith, having way more fun navigating together this crazy thing called LIFE than we would ever have apart. When we said our marriage vows before God, our family, and our friends, we made a covenant to stay together through thick and thin, knowing that life would bring challenges, but together we would face them head on, pray, and trust that the Lord of Lords was on our side.

The first few years of a pastorate at a new church have been called "The Honeymoon" phase. So we settled our honeymooning marriage into our honeymooning church in Rogers, Arkansas, a booming little town. Life was exciting. Life was good. We were newlyweds at a church that had just built a new sanctuary the year before we arrived. The people were ready to take the ministry of the church to the next level—hungry for leadership and new ideas. Chris rolled up his sleeves and got to work.

In fact, we were so in the honeymoon phase that four months after settling in, we were thrilled to announce we were expecting our first baby. Around the same time, our new friends Mark and Trish excitedly announced that they were expecting their first baby. Both babies were due the following September. Throughout our courtship, Chris and I had talked about having and raising children. We knew we wanted to "be there" for our children. I desired to be home with them for the first few years. The budget would be tight, but we agreed the sacrifice of a second income would be well worth the time we would spend nurturing our children and "raising them up in the way they should go" (Proverbs 22:6).

I was so thrilled to start my career as a "domestic engineer." You see, I was raised by a homemaker extraordinaire. My mom was a cookie-baking, dinner-making, homework-helping, chauffeur-driving, PTA volunteering, essay-typing, tear-wiping, laundry-folding amazing mom. My dad was a successful corporate executive who loved us, encouraged us, and worked extremely hard to provide for our family. Dad never allowed two words to be spoken in our home: "I CAN'T". My dad brought home the bacon and mom fried it up in the pan. My upbringing was my inspiration to be the best mom and wife I could be. When Chris and I first married, I couldn't wait to become a mom. I had anticipated having children for years and years. So when Emily was born, I started my "first career" called motherhood. This journey of parenting was my deepest heart's desire, and I enjoyed it tremendously.

My new friend Trish was a precious blessing to me. Together Trish and I shared the journey of first time pregnancy. We watched our tummies grow, lamented about morning sickness, shopped for baby items together, and even put the pen to the paper to determine how Trish could quit her banking job to stay at home with Joe after he was born. Joe would be her first and only child, and her heart's desire was also to be the one to nurse him, change his diapers, take naps together, and mold and shape his little life.

Trish became the closest of close friends. She never saw me as her pastor's wife. To her I was just Lisa, her friend. She was a true blessing that I was incredibly grateful for that during a potentially isolating time of being a pastor's wife in a new town, at a new church with a new baby.

Just a little while into Chris' pastorate in Arkansas, I began to notice an interesting dynamic I have learned is common among pastor's families. Friends, true friends, are hard to find. Now, I understand true friends can be hard to find for everyone, but being in ministry adds another dynamic that I will call "holiness." Everyone around the church wants to know and be known by the pastor...but just not too much. You see, when someone dares becoming close friends with the pastor (and/or family), that person risks allowing "the holy family" (yes, I have heard ourselves referred to in this way!) to see how "unholy" his/her life is. Then, of course, the opposite is also true. That person may see that the "holy family" isn't...exactly. Some things are left better alone...so when it comes time to go out to the lake for the weekend, the friends call their new neighbors instead of risking it with the pastor's family.

You see, there's a tendency for many people to put ministers and their families up on a pedestal and to keep them at arm's length. People tend to forget pastors and those in ministry are real human beings. Often times, those outside ministry naively want to believe their pastor and pastor's family don't have struggles or emotions or misbehaving children. It's easy to tell if someone is uncomfortable being themselves in the presence of a pastor or his wife - this person will apologize if a curse word slips as if we have never heard those words before nor ever accidentally used them! They have trouble just relaxing and being themselves. For some people, this gets better over time as our relationship with them develops. For others, it never gets better. That is why when Trish came into my life, she was a breath of much needed fresh air…100% herself from day one. I, in turn, was free to be myself. I knew I had found a friendship that would last a lifetime.

Lisa's Lessons from Shore

Do you put your minister's family up on a pedestal? If so, please take them down immediately. Call them up and invite them out to dinner. If they have young children, offer to babysit and give them a date night. When you see them at church, know that they feel a lot of pressure to be "perfect". Ask them how they are doing and then listen. Really listen. Be yourself around them so they will feel human and loved.

"For it is God who works in you to will and to act according to His good purpose."   *Philippians 2:13*

Chapter 4
Mom On a Mission

Chris was pulling long days at the church, and I was pulling long days at home. Families were visiting and the church was growing. Chris needed help. Within a couple of years our church called a dynamic associate minister to join our church staff. He was just out of seminary and full of passion, fresh ideas, and a willingness to join Chris in partnership. It was a match made in heaven, pun intended! An almost magical combination of which would lead our church into a time of growth it had not experienced in a long time.

Chris and I had an instant connection with Don and Laurie. They had no children yet, and we had just had our first child, Emily. Chris and Don saw eye to eye, both visionaries, natural-born leaders, deeply faithful with complimentary personalities. Laurie and I also had complimentary personalities. (This is just a nice way of saying, we were polar opposites!) However, this is why we clicked instantly as friends. Laurie was a go-getter, career-driven young woman just starting to pursue her master's degree in the health care industry. I admired her ambition, her career goals, her desire to develop her own career and identity as a pastor's wife. Laurie wasn't the "stay at home mom" type. We often laughed about our different upbringings but appreciated each other's strengths all the more.

Shortly after we found out we were expecting our second child Robert, Don and Laurie found out that Rachel was due just a couple of months later. Oh the fun our church had with both minister couples expecting babies around the same time! Joint baby showers, the buzz of joy and anticipation in the air, and lots of teasing comments such as "The minister's families really know how to grow a church!"

Two years after Robert was born we had Patrick, then five years later our little grand finale, Carol Ann. I poured my energies into our children, our home, and our ministry in the community. Most of the time, I absolutely loved being home with my babies and preschoolers, but some days were long and lonely. I am a people person and sometimes the isolation was discouraging and disheartening. Some days I longed to drop my children off at daycare and school like my friend Laurie and other career moms I knew and go into an office setting surrounded by other adults. I longed for adult conversation, intelligent discussions, problem solving outside of where my son's right tennis shoe could possibly be hiding or what could I make for dinner with an onion, a couple of eggs, and a package of frozen peas. After all, loading up four children and heading to Walmart was about as much fun as being stung by a jellyfish 10 times at the beach.

Out of that desire for social interaction, encouragement in the difficult journey called parenting, and the need for friends who understood, I helped start a ministry called Moms with a Mission. Mommies of pre-schoolers gathered together to encourage one another, laugh, cry, eat and just be on a mission to take a much needed break from our children for a couple of hours! Being in the presence of other women who were walking down the sometimes lonely and often frustrating road called motherhood was refreshing. We hired some nursery attendants, and gave our young children a chance to have a break from mom and play with their buddies in the church nursery. "Moms with a Mission" became our "Chicken Soup for the Mother of Preschoolers' Soul".

Lisa's Lessons from Shore

Is there a need in your community or church that you could fill? Are there others who are experiencing similar struggles or stages of life as you? There is a beautiful couple in our church who lost a teenage son in a tragic accident. They started a ministry called Grief Share, where anyone who is grieving over the loss of a loved one can meet together weekly with others and share in the healing process.

Life is about coming alongside each other and sharing struggles together, encouraging each other, and being a true friend. Life is about relationships, people, and lifting one another up.

"Therefore encourage one another and build each other up, just as you are doing"   1 Thessalonians 5:11

Chapter 5
Untying My Boat

At this point, I was a wife of one, a mother of two, and a friend to many. I was heading up a household and a few ministries. Our financial resources were limited while the need was great. I wanted to start a business--something I could work from home. So, when a friend approached me about a direct sales company offering a complete line of home and personal care products, I liked the idea and jumped in with both feet. This commission based business allowed me to work part time from home and make my own hours. I didn't have to punch a time clock or pay for childcare (we couldn't have afforded this anyway with four children!) Each month I struggled to meet the monthly minimum order, but I kept working it and learning something new every day. Occasionally my friends would host in-home gatherings for me to share my line of products with their sphere of influence. Chris and I worked around one another's schedules to cover the children...and our responsibilities.

I had a bent toward entrepreneurship, and I liked the idea of being in business for myself. Sure I was new and had a lot to learn, but I was up for the challenge. Life was full of children's activities, soccer games, gymnastics meets, Bible studies, Children's ministries, and... did I mention my family liked to eat? Meals, meals, meals—I could have spent my whole day just preparing, serving and cleaning up from meals. I was holding down the home front while Chris worked long hours at the church. Sometimes I felt like the juggling clown in a circus with parenting, ministry and my new business, but I was growing and learning and enjoying this challenge circus!

Owning my own business was not a foreign idea to me. My great grandfather, Jiddo (grandfather in Arabic) Abdullah left his homeland of Lebanon at 11 years old, arrived in this country through Ellis Island in 1902, and courageously made his way across America selling notions: small useful things (such as pins, thread, buttons) that are used for sewing. He eventually established roots in Hollis, Oklahoma. My great-grandfather instilled a work ethic in his children and grandchildren and even passed it to his great-grandchildren (that would be me and my ten first cousins).

My grandfather, the next generation, owned a grocery store and hamburger restaurant, before going into the insurance business. His wife, my Sitti Marge (Arabic for grandmother- pronounced sit-tee) and my great Aunt Josephine owned a women's apparel store in Wichita Falls, Texas. As a child, I remember the anticipation of driving to visit our big Lebanese family for a weekend or holiday. Krissy and I couldn't wait to get to "The Store", as we called it. We would spend the day watching my grandmother and aunt serve each customer with love and patience, helping them find the perfect outfit they were looking for. Each customer seemed to be a friend, and we listened to the conversations about children, grandchildren, spouses, and family stories.

The store had a bridal room in the back, and our favorite moments were spent watching a bride-to-be search for the ideal wedding dress. Krissy and I would wait in anticipation as the bride waltzed out of the dressing room looking like Cinderella adorned for the ball. These were magical moments.

My Uncle Tony, my Sitti's brother, wrote a book a few years back about their father's journey to America, called *Goodbye My Lebanon*. His dream to make a better life for his family and the courage he possessed to follow that dream in the face of great difficulties will always inspire me to take risks, to seek adventure, to live by faith.

Direct sales is a people business, and I quickly discovered that a quality that was modeled by my dad would be another tremendous asset in my new business. When it comes to people, my dad is the greatest. He can make a friend with anyone. He has a great big smile, and he makes it a point to learn peoples' names (a waitress, the guy at the tire store, anyone). He can make conversation with anyone on just about any topic. As a child and teenager, I watched my dad model this respect and kindness to everyone who crossed his path, whether that person was the CEO of a company, or a server mopping the restaurant at the end of the evening. He taught me to greet people with eye contact and a firm handshake, to call them by name, and to smile and spread some joy to their lives.

The company with which I partnered taught these same people skills. I was also encouraged to read books on leadership, personal growth, and financial independence. Of course, the greatest book ever written on personal growth and living a life of significance and success is The Good Book itself. I had spent years studying the Bible and quickly came to realize that the personal growth books I was reading came from that same source. I believe our Lord and Creator desires our personal growth and development more than anyone else. Faith is right in there too. God knows who we are and who He created us to be. Often we, ourselves, get in the way of the life God has for us to live. Our fears, doubts, egos, and selfishness weights us down and holds us back from His true purpose for our lives.

Well, there's nothing like a direct selling business to bring me face to face with some fears I had deep down inside. Sure, I was a people person, but making phone calls about church matters or play dates was one thing. Making phone calls to ask someone to try my products or to take a look at my business opportunity, totally different...and strangely scary! I constantly found myself in awkward situations, like when I would ask a friend to host a home party for me. I didn't like hearing the word, "No", I guess no one does. In my world, the word "no" coming from my toddler simply meant sending him/her to the time-out chair. What was I supposed to do with "No's" from grown adults? Now, rejection and hurt feelings were everyday occurrences. I didn't like it. How can this be that I am so excited about what I had to offer people, and they aren't? I just couldn't understand why others didn't see what I saw. What's the matter with these people?

In the early years of my sales and marketing business, I learned a valuable lesson that would prove to be crucial for me 15 years later. The lesson was this, "'No' doesn't necessarily mean 'no'. It might mean the timing just isn't right. I learned to quit taking 'no' so personally. 'No' just might mean—not right now."

As much as I loved people, the business was a struggle for me. One evening after we tucked the children in bed Chris said we needed to talk. I had been working this business for about five years part time from home without much success. "Ok here it comes", I thought. I had a feeling I knew what he was about to say. "L (as he calls me), I am so proud of you for the effort you have put into your business the past few years, but you have spent way more money than you have earned, and you have racked up our credit card balances trying to keep up with your monthly quota, personal growth tools, and quarterly conferences all over the U.S. I love your determination and your effort, but I think it's time to move on from this business."

My heart sank to the bottom of the ocean. I felt like a failure. I enjoyed the people I had met, the leaders who had mentored and inspired me, the goals and dreams I had developed. All my hopes came crashing down in an instant. It wasn't what Chris said. He simply told me what I already knew deep down. This wasn't the business for me.

Lisa's Lessons from Shore

During my first attempt in business, I attended a conference where a passionate leader exclaimed from stage, "Anything worth doing is worth doing poorly until you can do it well!"

Dr. John Maxwell wrote an incredible book entitled, 'Sometimes You Win, Sometimes You Learn". Have you tried and failed before? What did you learn from that experience? How are you a better, stronger woman through the failure? It's ok to throw a pity party for a few minutes. But they are really not much fun. There's no food there and no one comes to that party. So as Taylor Swift sings, shake it off, accept it, and move on. Your biggest failure could become a platform for a future success.

"Failure is simply the opportunity to begin again, this time more intelligently." Henry Ford

Chapter 6

You Don't Have To,
You Get To

Several years ago, when my children were young, I was having one of those deeply spiritual times with them around the dinner table. Chris was at church for a meeting, and therefore was missing out on this interesting, theological perspective shared with me that night by my children. We were talking about "worship." I was asking them, "What is worship?" and "Why do we worship God?" and "How do we worship God?" The final question's answer, really opened my eyes. I asked them, "Why do we go to church each Sunday?" All six of their eyes (eight, including Carol Ann, who was only a few months old and trying to participate in this deeply spiritual discussion from her bouncy seat) looked at me rather perplexed. My son, Robert, who was about 7 years old at the time, then piped up with an excited smile and very proudly blurted out the answer he knew was correct and said, "cause Dad's the minister! We HAVE to go!"

My face felt flushed. Where had I gone wrong in parenting these children? Did they truly think every time we went to church for anything it was because their dad was the pastor and we HAD to? If he had been an airline pilot, a coach, train conductor, a meter reader or a hot tub repairman, could we actually sleep in on Sundays? Had they missed the *"You don't have to, you get to!"* message somewhere along the way?

Chris brought this life lesson to the family from his days at Kanakuk Kamp, where the answer to any camper's question/complaint, "Do I have to?" was always met with this motto, "You don't have to, you get to!" Chris has been living "you get to" for years. For much longer than we have known each other, we have had a passion for youth ministry. We have had the privilege of working both separately and together with teenage youth at Christian summer camps, church camps, youth retreats, and weekly youth groups meetings. Chris directed the junior high church camp for 14 summers while we lived in Arkansas – definitely a highlight of his ministry. Occasionally, no, quite often, a teen would give him the whiny voice, "Mr. Pulliam, do I have to be her partner in this game? She doesn't like me." or, "Do we have to have lights out at 11 pm? That's too early." or, "Do I have to go on the hike? 'cause my legs are tired." His response was always, "You don't have to, you get to."

In our family, it's "Dad, do I have to help you with yard work right now? Do I have to clean my room today? Do we have to go to the early service? I'm tired!" to which Chris almost always replies, "You don't have to, you get to!" This motto overflows into many areas of life. Deep within these words is the idea that life is a privilege, that opportunity should be embraced, that hard work is good for you, that being in new situations outside of our comfort zones are the very things that stretch and grow us into becoming all God has created us to be. It is a privilege and an honor to be called a child of God. "How great is the love the Father has lavished on us, that we should be called children of God!" 1 John 3:1

Back at the kitchen table and our lively theological discussion about worship, I told the children it is a privilege to worship God freely and corporately each Sunday with our church family. We go to church NOT because your dad is the minister, but because we want to give God our love and devotion. This is ONE way we show it to Him. We want to be together with our church family where we can all lift our voices to praise His Name, to pray as one, to give hugs and handshakes, and smiles to the "great grandmas and great grandpas" who love you as if you were their own. If your dad was not the minister of this church, guess what? We would still go every Sunday – not because we have to, but because we get to!

I try hard to not fall into the trap of doing, serving, worshipping, and giving of myself, for the wrong motives. The motives behind my faith, must be and should equal the motives I would have no matter if I am a pastor's wife, an entrepreneur or any other role or profession. As a believer, I worship, I serve, I fellowship with other believers; I long for deeper relationships, Bible study and prayer because these are innate needs I have just because I am a child of God. God has lavished His love on me; therefore, out of my cup which overflows is my desire to love Him with my life. Steven Curtis Chapman sings a song called "I want to love you with my life." My role as a minister's wife, mom, business owner, Bible study leader, and youth ministry volunteer should not change the motives beneath my relationship with God.

I remember a wedding Chris was asked to officiate. I did not know the couple very well. The bride was the granddaughter of a member of our congregation. It was going to be a big wedding on a Saturday afternoon, and many members of our church were planning to attend. I would have to hire a babysitter because my children were still young, and I was in a dilemma whether I wanted to give up a lazy Saturday afternoon at home for this event. Several days before the wedding I simply mentioned to Chris my dilemma, to which he said, "Please don't come." Puzzled, I looked at him. He added, "I mean, come if you really want to, but not because you feel obligated."

The Bible reminds us to "do nothing out of selfish ambition or vain conceit, but in humility, consider others better than yourself." (Phil 2:3) As I checked my motive, I realized my struggle with attending the wedding was a "conceited struggle." As I looked honestly at myself, I realized it was my selfish ambition of wanting others to see that I was there, more than a pure motive of wanting to be there for the grandparents of the bride. I desired so much to have the stamp of approval of others, to have them look at me and say, "How did you manage to get away from that houseful of kids?! You just never cease to amaze us Lisa!"

"Man looks at the outward appearance, but the Lord looks at the heart" (I Samuel 16:7). Jesus is all about the heart. I love this about Him. I love that He sees straight through the exterior, and cuts to the quick.

Sometimes we "have to." There are responsibilities to fulfill that I don't always want to do, nor do I always have a good attitude about fulfilling them. Here's where a "you don't have to; you get to" speech to myself works wonders!—a reminder of who we are and whose we are…and that we must embrace the possibilities of life with an attitude that is pleasing to the One who gives us opportunities.

Lisa's Lessons from the Shore

Are you a people pleaser? I certainly am. I have struggled with this my whole life and still do. Are you saying Yes because you think someone else wants you to? Or because you truly feel that God is asking you to? What have you said Yes to that you are currently feeling frustrated or resentful about? How can you graciously say No, or change your motives and complete the task with joy?

My favorite verse from my favorite Psalm in all the Bible says: "Search me Oh God and know my heart. Try me and know my anxious thoughts. See if there be any hurtful way in me, and lead me in the way everlasting." Psalm 139:23-24

Chapter 7
Running On Empty

Have you ever flat run out of gas?? You are running along in your life trying to keep all the plates spinning, handle the kids, the home front, your job or business, your involvement in church or your community. You feel like you are running from one obligation to the next until one day you just crash and burn. You don't see it coming and it catches you by surprise. You are empty inside and you're spent. And one day you just lose it.

Chris and I had been a double Honda Accord family since our first year of marriage. We love Honda Accords. We felt cool in those cars. When you are a pastor's family, anything to help you feel cool is greatly appreciated. When our third child Patrick was born, there was simply no way that a third car seat would fit into a Honda Accord. So we set out in search of a larger vehicle: a van. Just a few years before minivans were exploding onto the scene, we found a gently used Chevy AstroVan we could afford. The impressive thing about this van is it held EIGHT people, double what a Honda held. When we stepped into it, we felt like we were in an efficiency apartment, minus the kitchen sink and washer/dryer! Topping off the impressiveness of the AstroVan's size, was its color. It was a cross between maroon, purple, red, and pink, depending on how the sun was glistening on it at any given time. The official color was listed as "Cherry Ice". Yes it was icy alright. The "cool" phase of our lives was definitely over. We had traded in cool for a van that all five of us could ride in at one time.

The most unique feature of the AstroVan, however, was the gas gauge. No matter how much or how little gas was in the tank, it always looked like the tank was two thirds full. So Chris taught me how to set the trip mileage gauge and instructed me to never ever let the trip mileage go beyond 250 miles. Ideally, I should fill up around mile 200 or 225. Some would comment, "Here's an idea. Why not just get the gas gauge fixed?" Answer: $600! That's why. Besides, all I have to do is remember to reset the trip mileage every time I fill up. "Got it, honey", as I gave him the thumbs up signal and thought, "What idiot would ever let the van get all the way to empty…?"

The first time I ran out of gas should have been the last. I was driving Emily across town to her gymnastics practice after school. Just before we turned onto the street where her gym was, the van started slowing down and losing all acceleration. Somehow, I had a hunch to pull into the middle turn lane with my left blinker just as our van halted to a stop. 'Seems like I just filled up the tank a few days ago…" I mumbled to myself. Did I seriously just run out of gas?

Would you believe there was a gas station to my left? Problem was, I couldn't get there. My three precious children sat quietly in the back seat, eyes as big as saucers (kids have a sixth sense when something is wrong, don't they?) as cars pulled up behind me waiting their turn to go left into the gas station, and cars to my left were speeding past us going the opposite direction. What was I to do? Lord, please help me.

As the honking behind me became deafening I looked in the rearview mirror and saw a huge pickup truck whose driver was no doubt wondering why I wasn't turning left. I waited for a break in the traffic, then jumped out of the driver's seat and jogged back to meet the anxious driver behind me. He rolled his window down, "Hello sir," I smiled kindly and timidly. "I apologize for the delay. I have a little bit of a problem .. ummm.. I ran out of gas and I need some help getting into that gas station right there," I pointed behind us. Could you give me a push?

Next thing I knew, I was steering the AstroVan slowly into the gas station being pushed from behind by a great big truck and a very nice gentleman.

The second time I ran out of gas happened about a year later along highway 290 outside of Houston. We had spent the week at the beach visiting my sister's family for the week. Kristen and her husband John are coastal people. They met, fell in love, and married while living in Galveston, a beautiful beach town on the Texas Gulf coast. And, with the exception of two of their married years, they have lived in south Texas near the water ever since. Some people are just meant to live near the ocean. They enjoy the spontaneity of taking their four children to the beach for a Saturday family outing, packing a picnic supper and hitting the beach for an evening oceanside sunset sandwich supper, or taking kayaking or surfing lessons just for fun. Their love for living near the water has enabled me to spend much more of my adult life digging my toes into the sand than I ever would have been able to do otherwise. As long as Krissy and John and their four children (affectionately called the Burks) live near the coast, we can make budget friendly beach memories year after year. When my brother John and his wife Katie join us with their two little guys, Trey and Tyler, the phrase "Fun in the Sun" becomes an understatement. Our ten stair-stepped children, cousins now ranging in age from 22 down to 4 years old, are as close as brothers and sisters, and have a blast every time we are together.

The Pulliam six had driven from Arkansas to the coast in the AstroVan for the much anticipated annual beach vacation with the Burks. The kids spent days alternating between building sand castles, throwing Frisbees, and boogie boarding with the dads while Krissy and I savored our much needed sister time. Since our teenage years, we have made a tradition out of lying in the sun, sipping Diet Coke, eating peanut butter M&M's and talking for hours.

A couple of days before our vacation ended, Chris and our son, Robert, left to return to Arkansas for a baseball tournament. Meanwhile my sister and I had planned a road trip with the balance of our children to visit our folks in Fort Worth. Kristen and her three children at the time, plus me and my three equals eight of us! We were excited that we would all fit in the Cherry Ice AstroVan. So we piled in and set out driving across the state of Texas toward Sitti and Grandad's house. We popped the Beach Boys CD in and resumed our sister time as the kids entertained each other in the back two rows of seats.

Somewhere around forty-five minutes into the trip, I felt the van slowing down. When I tried to accelerate and the opposite happened, my heart skipped a beat and my face started to feel flushed. I remembered Chris' departing words before leaving a couple days earlier, "Don't forget to keep an eye on the trip mileage…"

Once again, I was able to pull the van over to the shoulder of the highway, just as the van came to a complete halt. I can hear my sister's words like it was yesterday, "Lisa, are we running out of gas?" in a semi-panicked tone of voice.

"I am afraid so…" I leaned my head down on my hands which were still holding the steering wheel. How could I have let this happen… again?? It was bad enough running out of gas with my own children in the van last year, but now with my sister and her children traveling with us?" I wasn't sure whether to feel embarrassed, devastated, or just plain angry at myself.

We managed to get all the windows rolled down before the van came to a dead standstill. We looked at each other and, despite wanting to scream with fear, anxiety, and uncertainty, we decided to remain calm for the kids' sake. After a few deep breathes, the lack of air conditioning on this 98 degree sweltering summer day became very apparent. Cars were whizzing by us and no one was stopping. And did we really want anyone to stop with six children in our care? Unlike my first adventure in running out of gas, there was not a gas station in sight. Beads of sweat began rolling down my forehead and back. I knew the children must be getting hot too. We passed water bottles and juice boxes around the van...we waited, prayed and had no idea what to do next.

I heard my niece from the backseat ask Emily, "What's happening? Why are we stopping?" To which I heard a little voice reply, "We ran out of gas again. This happens all the time. My mom always forgets to look at the gas gauge."

It took every ounce of self-control not to turn around and yell, "What do you mean this ALWAYS happens??!! It's only happened once before! I look at this %&^$^*%@ gas gauge every single day!! But I reached up and clamped my hand over my mouth, looked at Krissy as if to say, *"I am about to lose it."*

Within a few minutes we saw a motorcycle pulling up behind us. An older gentleman walked around to Krissy's side window. "You ladies having car trouble?" he asked in a genuine voice with a Texas twang. "Well" ... I can't believe I have to say this again, I thought to myself, ... "we ... uhhh.. we ran out of gas."

"Well that's a simple problem to fix," the man replied, "I'll be right back." And before you could say Jeminy Cricket, that kind gentleman disappeared, and five minutes later was back and pouring a can of gasoline into our tank. He then told us to follow him to the gas station up at the next exit. We thanked him and thanked him and offered to pay him for his time and for the gas he had put into our tank. He would not accept anything from us. Before he rode away, he simply said, "Ladies, I have a daughter about your age, and she has young children, my grandchildren. And if she were ever stranded on the side of the road, I would hope a kind person would come along to help her. Have a blessed day," and he rode away.

Lisa's Lessons from the Shore

Running on empty is a dangerous place to be in life. This can happen when we allow busyness to distract us from the one thing in life that will make a huge difference. This over-busyness is draining to the soul and spirit as we begin to lose touch with ourselves and what God would have us do. Are you running on empty? If so, give yourself permission today to refuel your tank. Do whatever it takes: escape for a little while to your favorite beach, winery, lakeside lounge chair or coffee shop. Get outside and breathe in some fresh air and listen to your favorite praise song, the Beach Boys, or James Taylor. Put your toes in the sand and savor a few minutes of just being.

"As Jesus and His disciples were on their way, he came to a village where a woman named Martha opened her home to Him. She had a sister called Mary, who sat at the Lord's feet listening to what he said. But Martha was distracted by all the preparations that had to be made. She came to him and asked, "Lord, don't you care that my sister has left me to do the work all by myself? Tell her to help me!"

"Martha, Martha, the Lord answered, you are worried and upset about many things, but only one thing is needed. Mary has chosen what is better and it will not be taken from her." Luke 10:38-42

Chapter 8
Domestic Engineer to Entrepreneur

After fifteen years with our beloved church family in the beautiful town of Rogers, Arkansas, we were called to a new church in January of 2008. Our children were ages four to fourteen. They asked tearful questions such as, "Why does Dad have to go to a new church? We like the one here!" and "All of our best friends are here!" Chris and I prayed some heart wrenching prayers "Lord, are you sure this is from you?" The church family and ministry in Rogers had been our life for so many years. Looking back on the relationships we had shared, the celebrations of new babies and weddings, and the tearful embraces of those who had lost loved ones—our ministry here was wonderful. The people had embraced us and loved our children like their own. God had woven our lives together into an exquisite tapestry.

Now it felt like we were being torn away. To say this was an emotional and difficult time for the Pulliam six and the church family was an understatement, but we knew the Lord was calling us and therefore, we would follow Him. Despite the tearful goodbyes, a deep sense of peace accompanied us as we headed out on a new, "Great Adventure". We knew God was at work in our lives, and that is always a good place to be. So the house hunting began.

With Emily and Robert just entering their teenage years, and Patrick and Carol Ann following close behind, we needed more space. Chris's number one criteria was a big yard where he could throw the football with the boys. The kids' top request was "Can we each have our own room?" My desire was a beautiful back deck with, you guessed it, a swimming pool. I needed a place to dig my toes in the sand. I had also dreamed of a yard where we could invite family and friends over for grilling out and enjoying an evening under the stars. To top it off, while living in Arkansas, I had become recertified through Red Cross to teach swim lessons again and wanted to start a summertime business in our new town. The moment we saw "The House", we all fell in love. It was an older home and it needed a lot of work. However, there was a huge front yard for sports, all the kids would have their own room, and guess what the backyard had? Yes, you guessed it. A most beautiful deck and swimming pool surrounded by several palm trees. I was in heaven.

After we moved in, my life consisted of helping our four children get situated into middle schools, elementary school, pre-school, sports, orthodontists, church, youth group—you get the picture. The transition was tough at times, but our children slowly began adjusting to their new life and meeting new friends. By the time Carol Ann started first grade, the family was "transitioned"—all of us but one…me. I came face to face with a nagging feeling that had been hanging around my soul for several years. You probably know the question. It had been creeping up on me like the tide since before we moved to Texas…"What's next for me?"

As our fourth and final child, Carol Ann, went off to first grade that fall, I reflected on my life as I knew it. For sixteen years, I had been the mom of Emily, Robert, Patrick and Carol Ann, wife of Chris, "pastor's wife," PTA mom, soccer mom, housekeeper, chauffeur, cook, Bible study leader, and Youth leader. I loved it ALL. I was grateful for the years I had been able to be home with my children, pick them up from school, hear about their day, work on projects, bake cookies, go to soccer practice, and cook dinner. For sixteen years I had the privilege of perfecting the skills required to be a pretty great stay at home mom. Proverbs puts it this way, "She looks well to the ways of her household, and does not eat the bread of idleness. Her children rise up and call her blessed; her husband too, and he praises her" (Proverbs 31:27-28).

I don't think anyone was rising up to call me blessed, but I was good at domestic engineering. I was comfortable there.

Now, however, my children were sixteen, thirteen, eleven, and six years old, and a restlessness dripped on my soul that I couldn't seem to shake. A little voice inside of me was speaking to me, and its whisper was becoming louder and louder. *"It's time for you, Lisa"* is what I heard. *"It's time."* I had been developing my swim lesson clientele since we moved here the year before. Word had travelled quickly among mommies everywhere that a new swim teacher was in town! I thoroughly enjoy teaching children the necessary skills of swimming and water safety. However, it was a seasonal business, feast for three months and famine for nine.

I began searching out a variety of new careers. One night I was up late and saw a commercial on flipping houses. "Hmmm, that sounds fun," I thought. "Real estate could be a great career in this booming economy. Or how about becoming a teacher? I love children, and I would share the same schedule with my children." Still relatively fresh in my mind was the memory of how much I had enjoyed leading our Children's ministry at our church in Arkansas. I dug deep to explore each of these careers, but I just didn't feel a peace in my soul about any of them.

One morning after getting the children off to school, the backyard, poolside deck was beckoning me. With my mug of coffee in hand, I took my place in the big, comfy, lounge chair, and leaned my head back to marvel at the clear blue sky. It was a gorgeous fall morning. I listened to the birds welcoming me as I opened my Bible and began writing in my prayer journal. All the thoughts and emotions running through my mind at that time flowed from my mind through my pen onto the pages of my journal. I had been journaling since age sixteen, since the year I had committed my life to the Lord and promised to follow him. I leaned back in my chair, looked up at the heavens and said, "My husband's a minister, God, but who am I? Who did You create me to be? You've given me joy, strength, laughter and a love for people. I have been home for 16 years raising our children, and I'm grateful for that time. I wouldn't change a thing, but you and I both know there is more to my life than this. There has to be more to me than this."

That was the day I began writing this book, seven years ago. I never thought I would be a published author. I only wrote because writing is therapy for me…a cleansing process. Something happens when I allow my thoughts, prayers, joys and struggles to work themselves out on paper. The more I write, the more clarity I find. Sometimes, I even feel as though God has spoken to me through the words He has prompted me to write. Problems don't seem like problems any longer, difficult situations find solutions, and the gray skies turn to blue as I read God's word and journal my prayers to Him.

That fall I had begun substitute teaching at Carol Ann's elementary school and considering the possibility of going back to school to become a full time teacher, but the restlessness continued. One day, she and I walked into the house after a grueling day in a classroom with 25 first graders. Tired, exhausted and ready to put my jammies on and sleep until the next morning, Chris greeted me at the door and informed me that our friend, Coach Johnston, was coming over that evening to discuss a new business venture. After the day I had had, everything in me wanted to yell, Nooooooo!" and run upstairs and hide under the covers. Chris knew I was searching whole-heartedly for something, and he knew that together we were going to have to do something different financially if we were going to make it through this next decade of college tuition, braces, and "life" in general. Still, I was thinking, "Does all that have to start tonight? Is he serious?"

Sometimes the Lord has an interesting and unexpected way of answering a prayer. After supper, we sent the kids upstairs to do homework, and I prepared myself to listen to our friend's presentation with as much attention as I could muster. What I heard and saw, in that next hour, captured my entrepreneurial spirit in a big way. After our friend was finished sharing the details, we realized this was a business venture we could not pass up. The company was only three years old. It was based in Dallas (close by) and was rapidly expanding across the United States. The company offered a service everyone uses every day—an essential service that people pay for without hesitation every month. The opportunity was truly limitless.

At the end of the presentation, Coach asked us, "Well, are you ready to get started?" Chris and I looked at each other, smiled, turned back towards Coach and in unison said, Yes!" Chris told me he would maintain his focus on our church and being the leader God had called him to be there, but he would support me whole-heartedly in this new venture. In one swift decision, I went from domestic engineer to budding entrepreneur and CEO of my own company. *"Hurray,"* I think.

The next morning when my alarm sounded, the first thought that popped into my head was, "What have I said yes to, Lord?" My heart sank. Doubt and fear came over me like an impending rain cloud. A little voice was whispering in my ear, *"What do you think you're doing, Lisa? You have failed before in business, what makes you think this time will be any different?"* The voice was right. Flashbacks of my early attempts in direct sales bombarded me. I had tried so hard for five years and never made a dime. In fact, I had spent more money than I made! What was I thinking saying "Yes" to a business (industry) I knew very little about? Was I fooling myself to believe that I even had a shot at success in this type of opportunity?

I dragged myself downstairs, made some coffee, and put on a smile as my children came into the kitchen for breakfast. As soon as they were all dropped off at school, I returned home, sat down at my computer, and tried to figure out where to start with my new business. I didn't have a clue, so, I called Coach out of desperation, thanked him for the opportunity and then basically said, "help!" I asked him if he would give me some guidance and training. He said he certainly would, and then he gave me the first of many of his lessons, "You are in business for yourself but not by yourself." He reminded me that I have a team around me willing to offer support, mentoring, and encouragement. Whew! That was good news...really good news. He guided me to some online training videos that would begin to educate me on my company and the opportunity. His closing words were something like, "Take it one day at a time. Take positive action for your business every day."

The second lesson I learned from Coach was "Don't Fear Failure." Failure doesn't mean you are a failure. It just means you haven't succeeded yet. Failure means you are trying. You are untying your boat from the dock. You are saying, "Yes" and stepping out in faith. Failure means you are taking action...and when you take action, you learn something new, you grow, you gain more confidence, you increase your skills. J.K. Rowling, one of the best-selling authors of all time, said, "It is impossible to live without failing at something, unless you live so cautiously that you might as well not have lived at all, in which case you have failed by default."

The next four years that followed were checkered with failure. I heard lots of No's, lots of "I don't do those kinds of businesses," and lots of "now is not the time." So many people decided to pass on my opportunity and stay in their comfortable boat. I made a lot of mistakes. But somehow, this time was different than the last. Sure the "No's" were discouraging, but they also stoked a fire inside me to keep going, to keep picking up the phone, meeting with people, sharing my opportunity, helping other people begin changing their lives, and developing a strong marketing team. In fact, within three and a half years, I failed my way to the second highest leadership level of my company, Executive Consultant. At the time of my promotion in May of 2013, out of roughly 300,000 consultants across the nation, only 300 were Executive Consultants. Reaching this level of promotion was one of the greatest accomplishments of my adult life.

The third great lesson I learned from Coach and other great leaders in this business was this: "Just do it." Or in Coach Johnston's lingo, "Just Nike this bad boy!" I vividly remember several years ago, presenting my business over lunch a local restaurant with a roomful of consultants and guests. After the meeting was over, I began to pack up the projector and screen when one of the guests approached me with a question. She said, "You told us that your husband is a pastor of a church and that the night that both of you saw this opportunity you said yes and joined immediately" I replied, "Yes that's exactly what happened." She asked me, "Well didn't you want to take some time to pray about it first?"

I paused then looked at her intently, "We most certainly did pray about it. For the previous two years leading up to that night we had pleaded for the Lord to bring something into our lives we could work part time that would bring us some financial relief. The night we saw this business together, we knew without a doubt this was His answer to our prayer."

Lisa's Lessons from Shore

Sometimes the most incredible opportunity you have ever been offered is staring you right in the face. Will you recognize it? Will you say, "Yes"? Will you dare to get your pretty, pedicured toes out of the sand, dive in and start swimming as hard and fast as you can even though jellyfish are all around you and sharks are nibbling at your ankles?

I remember a quote I read a long time ago that said, "When you wake up in the morning, you have two choices – you can go back to sleep and dream your dreams or you can wake up and chase your dreams." Chase your dreams. You will never ever regret this decision.

Chapter 9
Are You Lisa's Husband?

I stood backstage at the Dallas Convention Center, my heart pounding out of my chest. In about half an hour I would be walking onto a stage and speaking in front of 3,000 people. I was pinching myself in disbelief that my business had lead me to this moment in time—a pastor's wife, a mother of four, a housewife. Four years prior, I had taken a step of faith and said, "YES" to an opportunity that would change both my life and that of my family forever.

Each year over Labor Day weekend, my company hosts its annual convention, a truly phenomenal and inspiring event. Following my recent promotion to Executive Consultant, I had been asked by our corporate team to share my "Why." This, so called *Why* comes in two parts: 1) What compelled me to start a business and launch my career as an entrepreneur, and 2) What underlying reason drove me to do whatever it took in order to achieve such success. I sat backstage and prayed, *"Lord, please calm my racing heart. Please bring the words to my mind I have practiced a hundred times and allow me to be a blessing to someone out there. 'May the words of my mouth and the meditations of my heart be pleasing in your sight'" (Psalm 19:14).*

As I finished whispering that prayer, I looked down at my cell phone and decided to send a text message to three of my four children (Carol Ann, my youngest, didn't have a cell phone yet). I texted, "Em, Rob and Pat, I am sitting here backstage at the Dallas Convention Center about to walk out in front of 3,000 people and share my "Why." I just wanted to remind you that YOU are my WHY. I love you all, Mom."

All three kids were in school that day: Emily in her sophomore year in college at Texas Christian University in Fort

Worth, TX, Robert in his senior year of High School, and Patrick a sophomore. Emily was the first to respond, "Mom, I am so proud of you. I am praying for you today. I love you." Robert responded next, "Mom, you rock! I'm proud of you!" I waited for a text from Patrick but nothing came in. About that time, I was called to the closer area backstage. Someone clipped a microphone to my lapel. I took a deep breath and hoped my heart's pounding would calm down.

I was introduced by one of our million-dollar earners in Ambit, and when I heard my name, I took a deep breath, put a big smile on my face and walked out on stage. I felt nervous but confident ... ok, confident may be a strong choice of words... Inside I could not believe this was happening to me.

The next few minutes were a blur. Yes, a few minutes was all I had to share my story and express the deep gratitude I felt for the opportunity to learn and grow and become more the woman God created me to be. I had just a few minutes to share my faith, impact lives, and inspire others to pursue their purpose with passion. But I did it! Chris videoed my talk from the audience. Later when we tried to watch his video, it was awful. He apologized saying he was so nervous, he couldn't hold the camera still.

When I walked off stage I felt an exhilaration I had never felt before. I remembered hearing Dr. John Maxwell comment on what he says to himself after "wowing" the people and walking off stage. He says to himself, "I was made for this." Well, I don't know if I "wowed" anyone, but I definitely felt like I was made for this! My dream-like state didn't last long for my second thought was, *"I hope Patrick didn't try to text me and get his cell phone taken up in class."* Backstage I pulled my cell phone out and saw his sweet text—better late than never. "Mom, I can't believe you're speaking in front of 3,000 people. Wow! I'm proud of you." I remember thinking, *"I can't either buddy. I can't either."*

Something was going on way down deep beneath the surface of my soul. I was in search of my own identity. For as long as Chris and I had been married, at every church function in the community, at the pool, at the ball field, at the kids' schools, my official titles of introduction were one of the following: "Chris's wife," "my pastor's wife," or "Emily, Robert, Patrick and Carol Ann's mom." Whenever I ran into a member of our congregation, I was never introduced as Lisa Pulliam, period. It was always, "This is Lisa, our pastor's wife." Don't get me wrong here, I am honored to be Chris' wife, a pastor's wife, and my children's mom, but each introduction made me wonder, "Is that all I am? Is there more to me than this? Would the real Lisa Pulliam please stand up?" Somewhere along the road of this roller coaster journey called Life, I had become so identified by my husband and children that I wasn't sure who I was aside from them. I am not saying that I had lost my identity, but was searching for a new significant purpose in a fresh season of life. Does that make sense? I wasn't sure where this journey was going, but I liked the direction I was headed. I was being stretched like never before and discovering gifts and strengths that I truly didn't realize I had inside of me.

I walked…no, I floated off the stage. My first big speech behind me, my glory moment, the clapping and cheering of the audience, it was difficult to hear over my pounding heart. "Surreal" is probably overused, but my experience up on stage was truly a surreal experience. Oh what a feeling of accomplishment. I was thrilled beyond belief.

After the session, the crowd filed out of the arena and into the surrounding hallways. As I stood there with my husband a few feet away, people began to press in all around me. People I had never seen before began introducing themselves, sharing their stories, and telling me how much they related to my journey—the feelings of inadequacy, the financial stresses, the struggles of parenting. So many people, one after another after another—I did my best to greet everyone. I shook hands, listened intently, and gave encouragement as I could. I will never forget those moments...some of the greatest of my life. God was doing something bigger in me and through me than I had ever imagined.

Here's the really fun part. Off to the side where Chris was standing, he, too, was greeting people and shaking hands (all that comes natural for a pastor). That's when I heard something that was literally like music to my ears (or sunshine on my shoulders!). I heard a gentleman ask Chris, "Are you Lisa's husband?" I glanced over toward Chris only to see him smiling from ear to ear and nodding his head and saying, "Yes, I am". I couldn't stop my own smile from creeping across my face as big as a Texas sunrise. *"Lisa's husband?"* I pondered, I have to admit, I really liked the sound of that! I had never heard those words before in my life (okay, with the exception of my 20th High School Reunion). "Lisa's husband" ...that comment, that moment would be written on the pages of my heart with a big black Sharpie marker. For the first time in my married life, I wasn't just Chris' wife or Carol Ann's mother. My new life, my new identity, the new ME had made a first appearance, and I couldn't wait for an encore.

Lisa's Lessons from Shore

When I said Yes to my new business six years ago, I had absolutely no idea what was in store for me. I didn't know if I would succeed or fail. All I knew was that I would give this business everything I had to give it. If I failed, I would fail trying, not quitting. When I said yes this time, I was All IN. All in to learn, to grow, to figure out how to be a leader. Early on in my career, I heard our CEO Jere Thompson Jr. speak on the topic of commitment. And I have treasured this quote ever since:

"Until one is committed, there is hesitancy, the chance to draw back, always ineffectiveness. Concerning all acts of initiative (and creation), there is one elementary truth the ignorance of which kills countless ideas and splendid plans: that the moment one definitely commits oneself, then Providence moves too. All sorts of things occur to help one that would never otherwise have occurred. A whole stream of events issues from the decision, raising in one's favor all manner of unforeseen incidents and meetings and material assistance, which no man could have dreamed would have come his way. Whatever you can do, or dream you can do, begin it. Boldness has genius, power, and magic in it. Begin it now."   William Hutchison Murray

Make a commitment. One time. Don't look back. As you swim the deepest ocean, you never know what is waiting for you on the other side.

Chapter 10
SUPER Woman

My favorite event of my year was only a week away—The Ambitious Women's Conference. I sat at my computer with a blank screen before me with a daunting task ahead of me. A few months before, I had been asked to present a session at the conference called "Life Balance for the Busy Mom Entrepreneur." I had joyfully agreed and was honored to have a chance to share any pearls of wisdom I may have learned along the way from raising four children while working my business for the past five years. At the time I was asked to speak on this topic, I admit I felt inadequate. Striking a balance between home and work had been something I had struggled with intensely since embarking on my journey as an entrepreneur, but I had embraced the assigned challenge and hoped to share something of value with other busy moms.

I remember my words to my husband just three months before on New Year's Day, "THIS YEAR is going to be our year, honey! I can feel it. Our kids are doing great, and my business is on track to reach new heights. We sold our three money-pit rent houses last year. My thoughts continued, "Our second child is successfully off to college. The church renovation is almost finished, and our church is on the brink of explosion (the good kind). This is going to be the YEAR of all years; I can feel it." Those were my exact words as I sat on the threshold of 2015.

To kick off the New Year in a powerful way, I attended a motivational, financial seminar with two close girlfriends in business with me, Judy and Debby. The January weekend conference was awe-inspiring. I returned home to my family with goals and dreams intact, ready to make this the BEST year ever. I was ready for whatever God had in store for me. 2015 was going to be BIG.

Unpacking my bags from the conference, I was standing in front of the bathroom mirror when something caught my eye. *Am I seeing what I think I'm seeing? Certainly not.* I reached up to my neck and confirmed what my bathroom mirror reflected: a pea sized lump on my throat. I stood there running my fingers over and over it as my mind raced back in time seventeen years ago. After the birth of my third child, Patrick, I had developed a lump on my thyroid called a thyroid nodule. With three children under the age of five, I had navigated, with God's help, the fearful journey called "what if?" A biopsy revealed the nodule was not cancerous. The doctor told me it was probably due to hormonal imbalances of having three babies in four-and-a-half years. After all, wouldn't that make any woman's hormones go wacko?

Now, seventeen years later, however, something was definitely wrong. No pregnancies or births to cause a problem this time. In fact, my youngest was now eleven years old. Chris held me as we prayed and asked the Lord for His guidance and healing for whatever was going on inside my body. Tears soaked my pillow that night for what seemed like hours as I battled a sinking feeling inside of me. I whispered to the heavens above over and over, "No, Lord. I don't have time for any health issues right now. This is supposed to be MY year, remember?"

The next day began my quest to figure out what was wrong with me and why this nodule was back. In the midst of being a mom, wife and entrepreneur, I began walking down the road of medical appointments; check-ups with my doctor, an ultrasound, lab work, and finally to the endocrinologist. At the same time I was walking through the world of traditional medicine, I was also doing my own research on the side. You see, I believe we are "fearfully and wonderfully made" (Psalm 139). I couldn't help but wonder *"Why is this happening, Lord? What is causing my thyroid problem, and what can I do to change it? What is my responsibility in regaining my health?"*

So, I was dealing with a thyroid issue in addition to my usual juggling act, but I was determined this would still be my year! Then my cell phone rang. The principal from my son's high school was calling and, let's just say, he wasn't calling to congratulate me on any of Patrick's achievements. Chris and I were asked to come to the school immediately and meet with the principal. With my heart pounding I called Chris and told him the news. The silence was deafening as we drove to the school. The silence and anticipation hung in the car like a dark cloud of an impending storm.

We walked into the office to see our son sitting with a somber look on his face. "Patrick tested positive on a drug test today," the principal informed us, "He has admitted to taking marijuana on a school trip. We have a zero tolerance policy when it comes to school sponsored trips." Patrick was in trouble, big trouble. He had just returned from an out of town basketball tournament. The team was doing great. Patrick was not. To say we were stunned was an understatement. The next half hour in that office with the principal was a blur. How one decision by one family member can change the course of an entire family's life. For the most part, as a family, we had dodged the big stuff. "Being in big trouble" was unchartered waters for us. Humbled and with our hearts just barely afloat, the three of us walked slowly to the car and drove off the campus never to return again.

The next few days were spent in tears, silence, prayer, and more tears. We sought counsel for what we were quickly realizing was more of a problem than we had even remotely imagined. How could this have happened to our family, to me? How could I have missed these signs? Have I been so busy chasing my dreams and goals, pursuing my career, building my success, and pouring into other people, that I neglected my own son? I questioned the mom I had been and the parents we were.

As I walked into church the following Sunday morning I wondered if I would be able to hold it together. What would church members think about us knowing we were having problems at home? We had moved him to that school (and spent thousands in tuition) trying to give him everything he needed to succeed in life. Now, in one really poor decision, all of it had vanished into thin air as a genie in a bottle. Walking through the fellowship hall, I felt like I had a neon sign on my forehead that read "Bad Mom." I smiled and said good morning to a few people as I made a bee-line to the coffee bar. A beautiful friend named Kaye was working at the coffee bar that morning. She smiled at me and unknowingly asked me how I was doing. I guess that was the wrong thing to ask because all of a sudden, Niagara Falls came pouring out of my eyes. Kaye took me in her arms and I cried on her shoulder. After 23 years of marriage and ministry, this was the day I learned the extent of a church family's grace, kindness, and unconditional love. Simply amazing.

The next few weeks were hazy, navigating our son's difficulties, and helping him get settled back into the school he had begged to leave 18 months before. We worked to get him the help he needed. Wise counsel was high on our list of needs. And, of course, I spent time down on my knees like never before, crying out to the Lord for His wisdom, strength and peace. I desperately needed them all. Was it still my year? I wasn't so sure.

I started this chapter with my opportunity to speak at the Ambitious Women's Conference. Life looked very different now than it did months ago when I had accepted the invitation to speak. So, sitting before my computer, just two weeks after the nightmare I stared at a blank screen void of any words to say about a topic that was as foreign to me as Jupiter and Mars: Life Balance…HA! Who am I kidding!?

The past few years flashed before my eyes, and guilt washed over me like a tsunami over an island. Had this business that was going to change our lives for the better gotten the best of me? All the time and attention away from my family, late nights at meetings…all the phone calls and email, was it to blame? I was chasing a dream I believed God had placed in my heart, a life that I so desperately wanted. I thought about the sacrifices I had made to reach the level of success I had attained. I thought of the people's lives my business was impacting for the better, the personal growth I had encountered along the way, stepping out of the comfort zone of homemaker and becoming a leader of people. I thought about all the evenings I was away at business presentations instead of home tucking my children into bed and praying for them. I thought of all the Saturday mornings I was up early and gone for the day at company trainings and events.

Balance, schmalance. Had my journey from housewife and mom to entrepreneur been all in vain? Had I been the cause of my son's struggle? Had I misread God's plan for me and my family? My journey over the past few years had been intense at times, no doubt about it. Most days, this question haunted me: Was I being the best mom, wife, daughter, and friend I could be while becoming a success, or was I just becoming a success in one area only to fail in another? How can I "take care of business" while caring for 4 children who are growing up so fast? Some days I felt like I needed to wear a cape around my neck with a huge S for "Super Woman" on it. Most of the time, I was exhausted trying to be everything to everyone.

Life balance…I'm supposed to teach a session on life balance? Lord, you surely have a sense of humor. I need to sign up for a full-blown seminar on this topic, not teach it! I have cried more parenting tears over the past few weeks than I have shed in my entire life as a parent. "Lord, help me please." I whispered a prayer, "What can I possibly share that will bless other women's lives?" I put my head down and cried.

What seemed like hours later, I sat up, and felt a peace wash over me. "Lisa," I heard Him whisper to my soul, "You are fearfully and wonderfully made. I gave you the four beautiful children you have. I gave you the capacity to love and nurture them. I gave you the gifts and talents you have used to build your business and impact people's lives with your story. I have you, your children, your husband, and your life in my hands. I know the plans I have for you, plans to prosper you and not to harm you. You will seek Me, and you will find Me when you seek Me with all your heart. Trust Me, Lisa. Love me with all your mind, heart, soul and strength. Don't look at the size of your problems, but rather look at the size of your God. I am FOR you, and if I am for you, who can be against you? I created you in my inmost womb. I have loved you with an Everlasting Love. Lisa, you are not Super Woman, but you are a SUPER amazing woman." (Jeremiah 29:11; Mark 12: 30; Romans 8:31; Psalm 139:14).

God's Word, His love, and His grace washed over me. Two weeks later, I stood with my friend and business partner, Blenda before a group of moms. The message? "SUPER Woman." We even wore capes with a huge S on the back and got a few chuckles from the group as we made our grand entrance into the room! We asked them if they ever felt like they needed a Super Woman cape to accomplish all the tasks and demands of any given day. I shared my raw story, as transparently as I could. I prayed for God to use it to His Glory. Here is why YOU are a SUPER Amazing Woman:

"SUPER Woman"

Seek a Life of Significance, not Success
What does living a life of significance mean to you? Define significance.

Unwavering in your TOP Priorities
Who and what are your Top 3 priorities? Write these down and post them where you can see them daily. Fight fearlessly to keep these three in the Top Three.

Pause Daily to Pray and renew your Passion & Purpose:
How and when can you make this reflective prayer time a priority in your day? Schedule it into your day and keep that promise to yourself.

Entrepreneurial Gifts and Strengths:
You are gifted with strengths and passions! What do you enjoy doing? What are you good at? What personal qualities do others compliment you on?
"I praise You because I am fearfully and wonderfully made..."
Psalm 139:14

Role Model for those Closest to You:
Whose eyes and ears are watching your every move, listening to the words you speak, learning from you daily? The people behind those eyes and ears are your most important audience. Treat them with care and kindness. Listen to them, encourage them to be all God has created them to be. Then trust God with the outcome.

The Lord has never been closer to me than He was during the darkest days of 2015.

Lisa's Lessons from Shore

When life is falling apart, and everything is spinning out of control, and the pieces are lying all over the ground, there is One who embraces us with His never ending love. When the tears fall like they will never end, we can rest in the Lord's great comfort and know that "He is near to the broken-hearted and saves those who are crushed in spirit." Psalm 34:18

Though He may seem a million miles away, He is nearer than you think.

Chapter 11
My Oasis

If I have a few days or a week to get away, I drive seven hours south where the breeze is salty, the ocean waves are soothing, and the sunsets take my breath away. I find the perfect chair and I dig my toes in the sand and reconnect with myself and my God. But if I am in need of "Toes in the Sand" time and I only have two hours to spend, I go to my favorite place in all of East Texas. When my soul needs time to reflect, my mind needs space to think, and my heart needs to feel whatever it needs to feel, I know just the place.

I discovered this oasis a few years ago—a sort of mini-vacation. Nestled in the rolling hills of East Texas is a winery called Kiepersol (KEE-per-saul). The story of the lovely family that owns Kiepersol only makes the wine better (read their book "The Story of We", by Pierre DeWet). The tasting room overlooks rows and rows of magnificent vines. Sometimes I go to write, sometimes I work, sometimes I turn my phone off so no one can find me for a couple of hours. Regardless, I always sip a glass of one of my many favorite red wines, made from their homegrown grapes, and spend time reconnecting to my Vine.

The most beautiful time to be there is in the spring and summer when the vines are heavy with bundles of green and purple grapes. In the winter the vines are asleep. They are scraggly brown twisted branches with a few dead leaves still hanging on. They have worked hard, grown, thrived and produced a harvest from which some of the richest and most delicious wines in all of Texas have emerged. They have done their job and now they rest. They sleep for the winter and prepare themselves for a new year of harvest. . As long as they stay connected to the vine, the branches will receive the nutrients they need to bloom and bud and reap another beautiful crop of grapes next year.

As I write today, I am here enjoying an unusually warm winter day at Kiepersol. A Scripture comes to mind as I stare at the brown "dead-looking" vines, barren of any fruit. In John chapter 15, Jesus uses the vine and the branches as an illustration of our own lives:

"I am the vine and you are the branches. If a man remains in me and I in him, he will bear much fruit; apart from me you can do nothing. If anyone does not remain in me, he is like a branch that is thrown away and withers; such branches are picked up, thrown into the fire and burned." John 15:5-6

As I read that Scripture, I think deeply about the events of the past year. A year that has held the lowest of lows and the richest of blessings. It's been a year of drought, sorrows and grief, and a year of harvest, joy and answered prayer. Through it all, however, He wrapped me in His warm embrace. He held me close as I stayed connected to the Vine. From this Vine, I received nourishment and life-giving peace though the storms seemed to try and drown me at times.

A few weeks ago, I was standing in the kitchen when our son Patrick, a senior in high school walked in the door from school. "Mom," he said, "I've been thinking." I turned toward him trying not to show how excited I was that he wanted to talk. "I'm going to start a business," he said with a smile.

"Well that sounds pretty cool," I responded with a positive tone in my voice, "What kind of business?" He went on to tell me that all of his friends were into hats, and that hats are really popular right now. So Patrick began sinking his creative and artistic skills into designing his own logo. A few weeks later, "Pat's Hats" was launched. Patrick went to work on his new business venture with a fervor unlike I have ever seen from that guy. My son, who one year ago was facing monumental personal challenges, has walked through the fire and come out on the other side. The Lord has truly done amazing things in his life this past year and I am deeply grateful. Patrick will be graduating from high school this spring and has big plans for Pat's Hats as he goes off to college next fall to study business. Pat is my entrepreneur.

My oldest daughter, Emily is now 22 and graduating from college this year with a degree in Marketing. Emily is my blonde "mini me". Everyone says we look exactly alike! She is an absolute joy and blessing in my life. She is passionate about her faith in Christ and enjoys mentoring Middle School girls. Emily will be getting married this summer to the love of her life. Remember the teary goodbyes we said to our dear friends and church family in Rogers, Arkansas? Emily was in eighth grade that year and she probably mourned our move more than any of our other children. Emily and a cute blonde haired boy named Brandon had a huge crush on each other in middle school. Once we moved to Texas, they lost touch for seven years. The Lord truly has an amazing way of bringing His plan to pass. Last year those two reconnected through their mutual friend Shelby, and let's just say, it was fireworks! We are so grateful for the love they have found and are eager to see what is in store for them as they start their life together and make their way in this world following after God's heart.

Robert is our second oldest child, in between Emily and Patrick. He is a sophomore in college this year, and we are incredibly proud of the responsible, mature young man he has become. He has a brilliant numbers mind with strong people skills and a tireless work ethic. He works full time in the accounting field and is working hard towards an accounting degree. Robert is one of those "work hard, play hard" types. Nothing will keep him from the Colorado Rockies if he sees a chance to go snowboarding. I believe that the Lord has incredible plans for Robert.

As for Carol Ann (we call her "C–A"), she brings us more laughter and joy than any child should be allowed to bring. She is in seventh grade and plays on the basketball and volleyball team at her middle school. CA was six years old when I launched my career as an entrepreneur, and therefore she really doesn't remember my life as a stay at home mom. One of the blessings of my direct sales business has been the flexibility of my time. I enjoy picking her up from school every day and sometimes I am even able to pull off a home cooked supper! She learned to do her own laundry much earlier than her older siblings (out of necessity), and she can cook omelets, quesadillas, and a mean batch of chocolate chip cookies!

I was working like crazy to finish this book when CA walked into my study and asked, "How's your book coming Mom?" I replied, "Great!" Then she asked me, "Are you writing about me in your book, Mom? After all, I am your most favorite and most wonderful child so I deserve at least a paragraph!" CA keeps us laughing and reminds us to not take life too seriously.

So this has been a year of soul searching, introspection, and asking myself and my God lots of questions - the year started with a lump on my neck. As I navigated those turbulent waters, I encountered a couple of huge waves. Sometimes it felt as though my boat was capsizing. I hung on for dear life, prayed a lot, cried a lot and persevered. The Bible says "The Lord is near to the brokenhearted and saves those who are crushed in spirit." Psalm 34:18.

In time, the waves subdued. The waters calmed, the skies turned blue again and the aquamarine hues of the sky and water blended in such a way that you cannot tell where one began and the other ended. The storms don't stay forever. They can pass just as quickly as they descended upon you, but the Lord will never let you go. You hang onto Him and He will hang onto you. You know what's crazy? He hangs onto us even when we forget to hang onto Him!

Expect blue skies to come again. They will come.

Lisa's Lessons from Shore

Mandisa sings a song called "Stronger" and I love the words of the chorus:

"When the waves are taking you under
Hold on for just a little bit longer
He knows that this is gonna make you stronger, stronger
The pain ain't gonna last forever
And things can only get better
Believe me, this is gonna make you stronger
Gonna make you stronger"

You may visit Lisa's website at
www.lisacarolpulliam.com
Or email her at lisacarolpulliam@gmail.com

Made in the USA
San Bernardino, CA
03 June 2016